# Ma[

### by Iain Gray

## Lang**Syne**
**PUBLISHING**
WRITING *to* REMEMBER

# Lang**Syne**

**PUBLISHING**

WRITING *to* REMEMBER

79 Main Street, Newtongrange,
Midlothian EH22 4NA
Tel: 0131 344 0414   Fax: 0845 075 6085
E-mail: info@lang-syne.co.uk
www.langsyneshop.co.uk

Design by Dorothy Meikle
Printed by Ricoh Print Scotland
© Lang Syne Publishers Ltd 2014

All rights reserved. No part of this publication may be reproduced, stored or introduced into a retrieval system, or transmitted in any form or by any means (electronic, mechanical, photocopying, recording or otherwise) without the prior written permission of Lang Syne Publishers Ltd.

ISBN 978-1-85217-263-3

# Maguire

**MOTTO:**
Justice and courage are invincible.

**CREST:**
A stag atop a ducal coronet.

**NAME** variations include:
  Mac Uidhir *(Gaelic)*
  Mag Uidhir *(Gaelic)*
  MacGuire
  McGuire
  McGwire
  Guire
  Guirey
  Guiry

*Chapter one:*
# Origins of Irish surnames

**According to an old saying, there are two types of Irish – those who actually are Irish and those who wish they were.**

This sentiment is only one example of the allure that the high romance and drama of the proud nation's history holds for thousands of people scattered across the world today.

It's a sad fact, however, that the vast majority of Irish surnames are found far beyond Irish shores, rather than on the Emerald Isle itself.

The population stood at around eight million souls in 1841, but today it stands at fewer than six million.

This is mainly a tragic consequence of the potato famine, also known as the Great Hunger, which devastated Ireland between 1845 and 1849.

The Irish peasantry had become almost wholly reliant for basic sustenance on the potato, first introduced from the Americas in the seventeenth century.

When the crop was hit by a blight, at least 800,000 people starved to death while an estimated two million others were forced to seek a new life far from their native shores – particularly in America, Canada, and Australia.

The effects of the potato blight continued until about 1851, by which time a firm pattern of emigration had become established.

Ireland's loss, however, was to the gain of the countries in which the immigrants settled, contributing enormously, as their descendants do today, to the well being of the nations in which their forefathers settled.

But those who were forced through dire circumstance to establish a new life in foreign parts never forgot their roots, or the proud heritage and traditions of the land that gave them birth.

Nor do their descendants.

It is a heritage that is inextricably bound up in the colourful variety of Irish names themselves – and the origin and history of these names forms an integral part of the vibrant drama that is the nation's history, one of both glorious fortune and tragic misfortune.

This history is well documented, and one of the most important and fascinating of the earliest sources are *The Annals of the Four Masters*, compiled between 1632 and 1636 by four friars at the Franciscan Monastery in County Donegal.

Compiled from earlier sources, and purporting to go back to the Biblical Deluge, much of the material takes in the mythological origins and history of Ireland and the Irish.

This includes tales of successive waves of invaders and settlers such as the Fomorians, the Partholonians, the Nemedians, the Fir Bolgs, the Tuatha De Danann, and the Laigain.

Of particular interest are the *Milesian Genealogies*,

because the majority of Irish clans today claim a descent from either Heremon, Ir, or Heber – three of the sons of Milesius, a king of what is now modern day Spain.

These sons invaded Ireland in the second millennium B.C, apparently in fulfilment of a mysterious prophecy received by their father.

This Milesian lineage is said to have ruled Ireland for nearly 3,000 years, until the island came under the sway of England's King Henry II in 1171 following what is known as the Cambro-Norman invasion.

This is an important date not only in Irish history in general, but for the effect the invasion subsequently had for Irish surnames.

'Cambro' comes from the Welsh, and 'Cambro-Norman' describes those Welsh knights of Norman origin who invaded Ireland.

But they were invaders who stayed, inter-marrying with the native Irish population and founding their own proud dynasties that bore Cambro-Norman names such as Archer, Barbour, Brannagh, Fitzgerald, Fitzgibbon, Fleming, Joyce, Plunkett, and Walsh – to name only a few.

These 'Cambro-Norman' surnames that still flourish throughout the world today form one of the three main categories in which Irish names can be placed – those of Gaelic-Irish, Cambro-Norman, and Anglo-Irish.

Previous to the Cambro-Norman invasion of the twelfth century, and throughout the earlier invasions and settlement of those wild bands of sea rovers known as the Vikings in the eighth and ninth centuries, the population of the island was relatively small, and it was normal for a person to be identified through the use of only a forename.

But as population gradually increased and there were many more people with the same forename, surnames were adopted to distinguish one person, or one community, from another.

Individuals identified themselves with their own particular tribe, or 'tuath', and this tribe – that also became known as a clann, or clan – took its name from some distinguished ancestor who had founded the clan.

The Gaelic-Irish form of the name Kelly, for example, is Ó Ceallaigh, or O'Kelly, indicating descent from an original 'Ceallaigh', with the 'O' denoting 'grandson of.' The name was later anglicised to Kelly.

The prefix 'Mac' or 'Mc', meanwhile, as with the clans of the Scottish Highlands, denotes 'son of.'

Although the Irish clans had much in common with their Scottish counterparts, one important difference lies in what are known as 'septs', or branches, of the clan.

Septs of Scottish clans were groups who often bore an entirely different name from the clan name but were under the clan's protection.

In Ireland, septs were groups that shared the same name and who could be found scattered throughout the four provinces of Ulster, Leinster, Munster, and Connacht.

The 'golden age' of the Gaelic-Irish clans, infused as their veins were with the blood of Celts, pre-dates the Viking invasions of the eighth and ninth centuries and the Norman invasion of the twelfth century, and the sacred heart of the country was the Hill of Tara, near the River Boyne, in County Meath.

Known in Gaelic as 'Teamhar na Rí', or Hill of Kings, it was the royal seat of the 'Ard Rí Éireann', or High King of Ireland, to whom the petty kings, or chieftains, from the island's provinces were ultimately subordinate.

It was on the Hill of Tara, beside a stone pillar known as the Irish 'Lia Fáil', or Stone of Destiny, that the High Kings were inaugurated and, according to legend, this stone would emit a piercing screech that could be heard all over Ireland when touched by the hand of the rightful king.

The Hill of Tara is today one of the island's main tourist attractions.

Opposition to English rule over Ireland, established in the wake of the Cambro-Norman invasion, broke out frequently and the harsh solution adopted by the powerful forces of the Crown was to forcibly evict the native Irish from their lands.

These lands were then granted to Protestant colonists, or 'planters', from Britain.

Many of these colonists, ironically, came from Scotland and were the descendants of the original 'Scotti', or 'Scots', who gave their name to Scotland after migrating there in the fifth century A.D., from the north of Ireland.

Colonisation entailed harsh penal laws being imposed on the majority of the native Irish population, stripping them practically of all of their rights.

The Crown's main bastion in Ireland was Dublin and its environs, known as the Pale, and it was the dispossessed peasantry who lived outside this Pale, desperately striving to eke out a meagre living.

It was this that gave rise to the modern-day expression of someone or something being 'beyond the pale'.

Attempts were made to stamp out all aspects of the ancient Gaelic-Irish culture, to the extent that even to bear a Gaelic-Irish name was to invite discrimination.

This is why many Gaelic-Irish names were anglicised with, for example, and noted above, Ó Ceallaigh, or O'Kelly, being anglicised to Kelly.

Succeeding centuries have seen strong revivals of Gaelic-Irish consciousness, however, and this has led to many families reverting back to the original form of their name, while the language itself is frequently found on the fluent tongues of an estimated 90,000 to 145,000 of the island's population.

Ireland's turbulent history of religious and political strife is one that lasted well into the twentieth century, a landmark century that saw the partition of the island into the twenty-six counties of the independent Republic of

Ireland, or Eire, and the six counties of Northern Ireland, or Ulster.

Dublin, originally founded by Vikings, is now a vibrant and truly cosmopolitan city while the proud city of Belfast is one of the jewels in the crown of Ulster.

It was Saint Patrick who first brought the light of Christianity to Ireland in the fifth century A.D.

Interpretations of this Christian message have varied over the centuries, often leading to bitter sectarian conflict – but the many intricately sculpted Celtic Crosses found all over the island are symbolic of a unity that crosses the sectarian divide.

It is an image that fuses the 'old gods' of the Celts with Christianity.

All the signs from the early years of this new millennium indicate that sectarian strife may soon become a thing of the past – with the Irish and their many kinsfolk across the world, be they Protestant or Catholic, finding common purpose in the rich tapestry of their shared heritage.

*Chapter two:*

# Patrons and protectors

**'Justice and courage are invincible' is the proud motto of the Maguires – a truly apt sentiment that expresses the fortitude and bravery with which the clan held sway for centuries as lords of present day Co. Fermanagh, one of the six counties of Ulster, or present day Northern Ireland.**

The Gaelic form of the name is Mac Uidhir, or Mag Uidhir, stemming from 'Odhar', meaning dun or brown-haired.

Odhar had been a popular personal name because it came from the celebrated St. Odhar, a personal servant to St. Patrick, who brought the light of Christianity to the Emerald Isle in the early fifth century A.D.

Odhar was killed after taking St. Patrick's place in a bid to confuse enemies who were pursuing them.

While, as we will find, the Maguires gained a formidable reputation on the battlefield, many of the name also appear to have been inspired by the Christian example of their namesake, Odhar.

So great was the Maguire hold on Fermanagh from the thirteenth to the seventeenth centuries that the county was actually known as Maguire's Country, and it was here that they acted as patrons and protectors of the Church – with five Maguires serving as bishops of Clogher-Pierce and one serving as bishop of Rossa.

The Augustinian monastery of Lisgoole, on the shores of beautiful Lough Erne and founded in the twelfth century, was protected by the Maguire lords, while the Maguire chieftain Cúchonnacht II founded a Franciscan abbey at Lisgoole in the late sixteenth century.

One particularly prominent Maguire ecclesiastic was Bishop Cathal Maguire, born in 1439 and who died in 1498.

A learned historian, he was responsible for the compilation of invaluable historical annals that were later incorporated into the seventeenth century *Annals of the Four Masters*.

The first mention of the Maguires in the historical annals of Ireland goes back to about the middle of the tenth century, and the clan is thought to have first arrived in Ulster from the present day county of Westmeath, in the province of Leinster.

This means that in all probability they had formed part of the mighty invasion force from the south that wrested control of Ulster from the rival tribal grouping known as the Ulaid.

This laid the foundations of the Ulster kingdom known as Airghialla, or Oirghialla, anglicised as Oriel.

Separate septs, or branches, of the Maguires were scattered throughout Fermanagh, but it was the imposing summit of Cuilcagh, on the borders of Fermanagh and Co. Cavan, that was the site of the solemn inauguration ceremonies of the Maguire chieftains, in addition to a site known as Sciath Gabhra, near present day Lisknaskea.

One of the most significant events in Ireland's turbulent history was the Cambro-Norman invasion of the late twelfth century, leading as it did to the consolidation of the power of the English Crown over the island.

No native Irish clan, least of all the Maguires, was immune from the consequences of the invasion.

Twelfth century Ireland was far from being a unified nation, split up as it was into territories ruled over by squabbling chieftains who ruled as kings in their own right – and this inter-clan rivalry worked to the advantage of the invaders.

In a series of bloody conflicts one chieftain, or king, would occasionally gain the upper hand over his rivals, and by 1156 the most powerful was Muirchertach MacLochlainn, king of the O'Neills, who along with the Maguires were among the most influential of the Ulster families.

Rory O'Connor, king of the province of Connacht, opposed MacLochlainn, but he increased his power and influence by allying himself with Dermot MacMurrough, king of Leinster.

MacLochlainn and MacMurrough were aware that the main key to the kingdom of Ireland was the thriving trading port of Dublin that had been established by invading Vikings, or Ostmen, in 852 A.D.

Dublin was taken by the combined forces of the Leinster and Connacht kings, but when MacLochlainn died the Dubliners rose up in revolt and overthrew the unpopular MacMurrough.

A triumphant Rory O'Connor entered Dublin and was later inaugurated as Ard Rí, but MacMurrough was not one to humbly accept defeat.

He appealed for help from England's Henry II in unseating O'Connor, an act that was to radically affect the future course of Ireland's fortunes.

The English monarch agreed to help MacMurrough, but distanced himself from direct action by delegating his Norman subjects in Wales with the task.

These ambitious and battle-hardened barons and knights had first settled in Wales following the Norman Conquest of England in 1066 and, with an eye on rich booty, plunder, and lands, were only too eager to obey their sovereign's wishes and furnish MacMurrough with aid.

MacMurrough crossed the Irish Sea to Bristol, where he rallied powerful barons such as Robert Fitzstephen and Maurice Fitzgerald to his cause, along with Gilbert de Clare, Earl of Pembroke, also known as Strongbow.

The mighty Norman war machine soon moved into action, and so fierce and disciplined was their onslaught on the forces of Rory O'Connor and his allies that by 1171 they had re-captured Dublin, in the name of MacMurrough, and other strategically important territories.

But a nervous Henry II began to take cold feet over the venture, realising that he may have created a rival in the form of a separate Norman kingdom in Ireland.

Accordingly, he landed on the island, near Waterford, at the head of a large army in October of 1171 with the aim of curbing the power of his Cambro-Norman barons.

Protracted war between the king and his barons was averted, however, when the barons submitted to the royal will, promising homage and allegiance in return for holding the territories they had conquered in the king's name.

Henry also received the reluctant submission and homage of many of the native Irish clans – but not the proud Ulster clans such as the Maguires, who for many years would prove particularly tenacious in resisting the encroachment on their ancient lands and privileges of the English Crown.

English dominion over Ireland was ratified through the Treaty of Windsor of 1175, under the terms of which Rory O'Connor, for example, was allowed to rule territory unoccupied by the Normans in the role of a vassal of the king.

Three separate Irelands had been created.

These were the territories of the privileged and powerful Norman barons and their retainers, the Ireland of the disaffected Gaelic-Irish such as the Maguires who held lands unoccupied by the Normans, and the Pale – comprised of Dublin itself and a substantial area of its environs ruled over by an English elite.

A simmering cauldron of discontent and resentment had been created – one that would boil over periodically in subsequent centuries with particularly dire consequences for the Maguires and other Irish clans.

Ireland groaned under a weight of oppression that was directed in the main against native Irish clans such as the Maguires.

An indication of the harsh treatment meted out to them can be found in a desperate plea sent to Pope John XII by Roderick O'Carroll of Ely, Donald O'Neil of Ulster, and a number of other Irish chieftains in 1318.

They stated: 'As it very constantly happens, whenever an Englishman, by perfidy or craft, kills an Irishman, however noble, or however innocent, be he clergy or layman, there is no penalty or correction enforced against the person who may be guilty of such wicked murder.

'But rather the more eminent the person killed and the higher rank which he holds among his own people, so much more is the murderer honoured and rewarded by the English, and not merely by the people at large, but also by the religious and bishops of the English race.'

This appeal to the Pope had little effect on what became the increasingly harsh policy of the occupying English Crown against the native Irish such as the Maguires.

*Chapter three:*
# In freedom's cause

**An insidious policy known as 'plantation', the settling of loyal subjects of the Crown on the lands held by intransigent native Irish such as the Maguires, had started during the reign from 1491 to 1547 of Henry VIII, whose Reformation effectively outlawed the established Roman Catholic faith throughout his dominions.**

This settlement of loyal Protestants in Ireland continued throughout the subsequent reigns of Elizabeth I, James I (James VI of Scotland), and Charles I.

It was a policy that was fiercely resisted by the Maguires and other clans, who came to realise that the only way to combat it was by sinking their own differences and uniting in the face of the common foe.

It is in such times that heroes arise, and among their number was the legendary freedom fighter Hugh Maguire, Lord of Fermanagh, who played a formative role in the rebellion against Crown authority from 1594 to 1603 that is known to Irish history as Cogadh na Naoi mBliama, or the Nine Years War.

Before the start of the rebellion proper, however, Hugh Maguire had already proven to be a significant thorn in the flesh to the authorities.

His territory of winding rivers and forests had made him

near impregnable to assault from outside, but in 1586 a successful attempt was made and Maguire was forced to surrender and pledge an oath of loyalty to the Crown.

But no sooner had he taken on the mantle of chief of the Maguires following the death of his father in 1589, than he was back on the rampage – carrying out a campaign of guerrilla warfare from bases on the islands of Lough Erne.

Maguire besieged the Crown-appointed sheriff of Fermanagh and a body of his men in a church in 1590, and it was only through the timely intervention of Hugh O'Neill, 2nd Earl of Tyrone, who reasoned with Maguire, that the sheriff and his men were not slaughtered on the spot.

Maguire was nevertheless declared a traitor and a mighty invasion force under the command of Lord Deputy Sir William Fitzwilliam was assembled and descended on Fermanagh.

The force managed to take Enniskillen and the bold Maguire's response was to launch a counter-invasion into the province of Connacht.

It was here that he clashed with an army under the command of Sir Richard Bingham, president of the province of Connacht, at the battle of Sciath na Feart, near Tulsk.

It was a confusing encounter, fought under a blanket of dense fog, with both sides barely able to distinguish friend from foe.

The Crown forces fled the field but later regrouped and pursued Maguire and his men. But by this time he was well on his way back to his home territory of Fermanagh, he and his jubilant followers ladened with the rich booty they had plundered from Bingham's camp.

Allied with the equally legendary Hugh Roe O'Donnell, better known as Red Hugh, Maguire besieged what had now become the English garrison of Enniskillen in the summer of 1594.

Sir Richard Bingham attempted to relieve the garrison, but he was intercepted by Maguire and Red Hugh at the Arney River and soundly defeated at what is curiously known as Beal Atha na mBriosgaidh, or the battle of the Biscuits.

By the following year the Nine Years War had begun, first sparked off in Ulster but later spreading to other provinces.

Hugh Maguire was involved in the defeat of an English force at the battle of Clontibert in that year, while in 1598 he was one of the commanders at the battle of the Yellow Ford, where the English army was defeated and his old foe Sir Richard Bingham killed.

Maguire's rampages continued, raiding the province of Thomond in 1599 and helping Red Hugh O'Donnell to take the strategically important Inchiquin Castle, while he also had the command of Hugh O'Neill's feared cavalry as it swept like a storm through the provinces of Munster and Leinster.

The great freedom fighter's end finally came in February of 1600 when he and a small band were intercepted near Cork by a much stronger force under the command of Sir Warham St. Leger and Sir Henry Power.

Maguire, undaunted, spurred his horse into their midst, but received a fatal pistol wound from St. Leger.

Before he died, however, he summoned up enough strength to raise his mighty sword and cleave St. Leger's head through his helmet.

Hugh Maguire passed not only into family legend but also into Irish legend.

The *Annals of the Four Masters* said of him: ' He was the bulwark of valour and prowess, the shield of protection and shelter, the tower of support and defence, and the pillar of the hospitality and achievements of Oirghialla and of almost all the Irish of his time.'

Following their defeat at the battle of Kinsale in 1601 and the final suppression of the rebellion three years later in Ulster, the future of its leaders hung by a precarious thread.

In September of 1607, in what is known as The Flight of the Earls, Hugh O'Neill, 2nd Earl of Tyrone and Rory O'Donnell, 1st Earl of Tyrconnel, sailed into foreign exile from the village of Rathmullan, on the shore of Lough Swilly, in Co. Donegal, accompanied by ninety loyal followers.

Among their number was Hugh Maguire's younger brother Cúchonnacht, who is thought to have arranged for the ship in which they sailed from their native land.

He died in Genoa less than a year later.

Following the devastations that came in the wake of the invasion of Ireland in 1649 of England's 'Lord Protector' Oliver Cromwell, the final death knell of the ancient Gaelic order of proud native Irish clans such as the Maguires was sounded.

This was in the form of what is known in Ireland as Cogadh an Dá Rí, or The War of the Two Kings.

Also known as the Williamite War in Ireland or the Jacobite War in Ireland, it was sparked off in 1688 when the Stuart monarch James II (James VII of Scotland) was deposed and fled into exile in France.

The Protestant William of Orange and his wife Mary (ironically a daughter of James II) were invited to take up the thrones of Scotland, Ireland, and England – but James still had significant support in Ireland.

His supporters were known as Jacobites, and among them was Colonel Cúchonnacht Maguire.

Following the arrival in England of William and Mary from Holland, Richard Talbot, 1st Earl of Tyrconnell and James's Lord Deputy in Ireland, assembled an army loyal to the Stuart cause.

The aim was to garrison and fortify the island in the name of James and quell any resistance.

Londonderry, or Derry, proved loyal to the cause of William of Orange, or William III as he had become, and managed to hold out against a siege that was not lifted until July 28, 1689.

James, with the support of troops and money supplied by Louis XIV of France, had landed at Kinsale in March of 1689 and joined forces with his Irish supporters.

A series of military encounters followed, culminating in James's defeat by an army commanded by William at the battle of the Boyne on July 12, 1689.

James fled again into French exile, never to return, while another significant Jacobite defeat occurred in July of 1691 at the battle of Aughrim – with about half their army killed on the field, wounded, or taken prisoner.

Among the dead was Colonel Cúchonnacht Maguire, who had raised a regiment for the Jacobite cause after mortgaging a large proportion of his estates.

One of his loyal officers cut off his head and, stowing it in a bag, managed to flee the field of carnage.

He is said to have ridden day and night until he reached the Maguire burial ground on the island of Devenish, where the colonel's head was reverently interred beside his ancestors.

The Williamite forces besieged Limerick and the Jacobites were forced into surrender in September of 1691.

A peace treaty, known as the Treaty of Limerick followed, under which those Jacobites willing to swear an oath of loyalty to William were allowed to remain in their native land.

Those reluctant to do so, including many native Irish such as the Maguires, were allowed to seek exile on foreign shores – but their ancient homelands were lost to them forever.

A further flight overseas occurred following an abortive rebellion in 1798, while Maguires were among the many thousands of Irish who were forced to seek a new life many thousands of miles from their native land during the famine known as The Great Hunger, caused by a failure of the potato crop between 1845 and 1849.

But in many cases Ireland's loss of sons and daughters such as the Maguires was to the gain of those equally proud nations in which they settled.

*Chapter four:*
# On the world stage

**Generations of Maguires have flourished at an international level in a colourful range of pursuits, not least in the world of entertainment.**

Born in 1975 in Santa Monica, California, **Tobey Maguire** is the actor who has starred in the role of Peter Parker in the *Spider-Man* series of films, while **George Maguire**, born in 1990, is the English actor and Olivier Award recipient who was one of the three original cast members who carried the title role in the multi-award winning *Billy Elliot the Musical*.

**Gerard Maguire**, born in 1945, is the popular Australian actor best known for his role as deputy governor Jim Fletcher in the television series *Prisoner*, while **Sharon Maguire** is the British film director and writer who directed the 2001 *Bridget Jones's Diary*.

Born in 1952, **Jeff Maguire** is the American screenwriter particularly famed for his skill as a writer of film scripts with a sporting theme.

He wrote the script for the 1981 *Escape to Victory*, while in 2006 he provided the script for *Gridiron Gang*.

It was for a film without a sporting theme, however, that he received an Oscar for Best Original Screenplay. This was for the 1993 *In the Line of Fire*, starring Clint Eastwood.

Born in 1976 in Ilford, Essex, **Sean Maguire** is the English singer and actor who first rose to fame as a character in the popular British television children's drama *Grange Hill*. In America, he is best known for his role as Kyle Lendo in the CBS sitcom *The Class*.

In the world of music **Hugh Maguire**, born in Dublin in 1927, is the world-renowned violinist who has played for a number of leading orchestras, including the London Symphony Orchestra and the BBC Symphony Orchestra.

He also holds a number of posts, including artistic director of the Irish Youth Orchestra, violin tutor to the National Youth Orchestra of Great Britain, and professor at the Royal Academy of Music in London.

Born in 1969 in York, Pennsylvania, **Martie Maguire** is the American country music songwriter, instrumentalist, and singer who was one of the founding members of the Grammy Award-winning country music band the Dixie Chicks.

She was born Martha Glenor Erwin and took the Maguire name through her marriage in 2001 to Gareth Maguire, from Carnlough, in Co. Antrim.

In the world of books **Gregor Maguire**, born in 1954 in Albany, New York, is the author and board member of America's National Children's Book and Literary Alliance who is best known for novels such as *Wicked: The Life and Times of the Wicked Witch of the West*, and *Confessions of an Ugly Stepsister*.

Born in 1976 **Emily Maguire** is the Australian

journalist and novelist whose first novel, the 2004 *Taming the Beast*, was nominated for the prestigious Dylan Thomas Prize.

In the world of politics no less than three Maguires have achieved distinction as mayors of cities.

Born in Toronto in 1876 **Charles A. Maguire** served as mayor of the city from 1922 to 1923.

A former vice-president of the Hydro-Electric Railway Association, during his tenure as mayor he was largely responsible for major programmes that included street extensions, low tax rates, the building of a railway viaduct on the water front and general city improvements.

Born in Omagh in 1796 and later emigrating from Ireland to America, **George Maguire** entered politics and became the first foreign-born mayor and first Democrat to be elected mayor of St. Louis, in Missouri.

Back in Ireland **John Francis Maguire**, born in 1815 in Cork, was the lawyer, politician, businessman, publisher, and philanthropist who served as mayor of Cork on four occasions.

Founder of the *Cork Examiner* newspaper, he also travelled widely throughout the United States and Canada and wrote on Irish immigrants to these countries.

Born in Manitoba in 1949, **Larry Maguire** is, at the time of writing, deputy leader of the Progressive Conservative Party of Manitoba and the owner and operator of Maguire Farms.

**Thomas Maguire**, born in Philadelphia in 1776, was the priest who moved to Quebec, in Canada, and became famous for his dedication to the expansion of the French language, while **Father Bob Maguire**, born in 1935, is the Australian priest and community worker from South Melbourne who was awarded the Order of Australia in 1989.

Maguires have been, and continue to be, particularly active in the highly competitive world of sport.

Born in Glasgow in 1981, **Stephen Maguire** is the Scottish professional snooker player who in 2007 reached the semi-finals of the World Snooker Championship, only to lose to fellow Scot John Higgins.

In Gaelic football **Sam Maguire**, born near Dunmanway, Co. Cork in 1879 and who died in 1927, was the Gaelic footballer and Irish Republican who gave his name to the **Sam Maguire Cup**, the trophy given annually to the All-Ireland Senior Champions of Gaelic football.

In contemporary European football **Chris Maguire**, born in 1989 in Bellshill, Lanarkshire is the Scottish professional player who, at the time of writing, plays for Scottish Premier League club Aberdeen, while **Darragh Maguire**, born in 1967 in Dublin, is the Irish player who, at the time of writing, plays for St. Patrick's Athletic in the Eircom League Premier Division.

Born in 1980 in Sydney, **Joshua Maguire** is the Australian football player who has played for the New Zealand Knights.

In baseball, **Jack Maguire**, born in St. Louis, Missouri, in 1925 and who died in 2001, was the renowned Major League player who played for teams that included the New York Giants and the Pittsburgh Pirates.

On the cricket pitch, **John Maguire**, born in 1956 in Murwillumbah, New South Wales, is the former Australian cricketer who played in three Tests from 1983 to 1984.

In the military sphere, **Vice Admiral Joseph Maguire**, from Brooklyn, New York, is the former commander of America's Naval Special Warfare Command who, in July of 2007 was appointed to the post of Deputy Director for Strategic Operational Planning for the National Counterterrorism Center.

Still in the rather murky world of terrorism, the **Molly Maguires** was the name given to a feared secret organisation that originated in rural Ireland in the eighteenth century and later appeared in the anthracite coal fields of Pennsylvania in late nineteenth century America.

Along with other secret societies in Ireland such as the Peep O' Day Boys and the Whiteboys, the Molly Maguires engaged in violence and sabotage against the highly unpopular rural 'reforms' of landlords – reforms that left many families homeless and destitute.

There are several theories as to the origin of the name: 'Molly' may have been the owner of an illicit drinking den where members of the secret society met or even one of their members.

Another theory is that 'Molly Maguire' was a widow who had been evicted from her humble home and who inspired the formation of the movement in the first place as a means of seeking vengeance.

Widespread industrial unrest in the coalfields of Pennsylvania led to a number of sensational trials between 1876 and 1878 with the Molly Maguires accused of a catalogue of crimes ranging from intimidation and assault to robbery, arson, sabotage, and murder.

This was at a time when workers were simply seeking better working conditions from their powerful employers, and doubt exists to this day just how organised they really were and how much some of the evidence against them was 'framed.'

One theory goes so far as to maintain that, as an organised body in America, the 'Molly Maguires' were a figment of the imaginations of the mine owners and the Pinkerton Detective Agency.

Starring Sean Connery and Richard Harris, *The Molly Maguires* was released as a film in 1970.

## *Key dates in Ireland's history from the first settlers to the formation of the Irish Republic:*

| | |
|---|---|
| **circa 7000 B.C.** | Arrival and settlement of Stone Age people. |
| **circa 3000 B.C.** | Arrival of settlers of New Stone Age period. |
| **circa 600 B.C.** | First arrival of the Celts. |
| **200 A.D.** | Establishment of Hill of Tara, Co. Meath, as seat of the High Kings. |
| **circa 432 A.D.** | Christian mission of St. Patrick. |
| **800-920 A.D.** | Invasion and subsequent settlement of Vikings. |
| **1002 A.D.** | Brian Boru recognised as High King. |
| **1014** | Brian Boru killed at battle of Clontarf. |
| **1169-1170** | Cambro-Norman invasion of the island. |
| **1171** | Henry II claims Ireland for the English Crown. |
| **1366** | Statutes of Kilkenny ban marriage between native Irish and English. |
| **1529-1536** | England's Henry VIII embarks on religious Reformation. |
| **1536** | Earl of Kildare rebels against the Crown. |
| **1541** | Henry VIII declared King of Ireland. |
| **1558** | Accession to English throne of Elizabeth I. |
| **1565** | Battle of Affane. |
| **1569-1573** | First Desmond Rebellion. |
| **1579-1583** | Second Desmond Rebellion. |
| **1594-1603** | Nine Years War. |
| **1606** | Plantation' of Scottish and English settlers. |
| **1607** | Flight of the Earls. |
| **1632-1636** | Annals of the Four Masters compiled. |
| **1641** | Rebellion over policy of plantation and other grievances. |
| **1649** | Beginning of Cromwellian conquest. |
| **1688** | Flight into exile in France of Catholic Stuart monarch James II as Protestant Prince William of Orange invited to take throne of England along with his wife, Mary. |
| **1689** | William and Mary enthroned as joint monarchs; siege of Derry. |
| **1690** | Jacobite forces of James defeated by William at battle of the Boyne (July) and Dublin taken. |

# Key dates

| | |
|---|---|
| **1691** | Athlone taken by William; Jacobite defeats follow at Aughrim, Galway, and Limerick; conflict ends with Treaty of Limerick (October) and Irish officers allowed to leave for France. |
| **1695** | Penal laws introduced to restrict rights of Catholics; banishment of Catholic clergy. |
| **1704** | Laws introduced constricting rights of Catholics in landholding and public office. |
| **1728** | Franchise removed from Catholics. |
| **1791** | Foundation of United Irishmen republican movement. |
| **1796** | French invasion force lands in Bantry Bay. |
| **1798** | Defeat of Rising in Wexford and death of United Irishmen leaders Wolfe Tone and Lord Edward Fitzgerald. |
| **1800** | Act of Union between England and Ireland. |
| **1803** | Dublin Rising under Robert Emmet. |
| **1829** | Catholics allowed to sit in Parliament. |
| **1845-1849** | The Great Hunger: thousands starve to death as potato crop fails and thousands more emigrate. |
| **1856** | Phoenix Society founded. |
| **1858** | Irish Republican Brotherhood established. |
| **1873** | Foundation of Home Rule League. |
| **1893** | Foundation of Gaelic League. |
| **1904** | Foundation of Irish Reform Association. |
| **1913** | Dublin strikes and lockout. |
| **1916** | Easter Rising in Dublin and proclamation of an Irish Republic. |
| **1917** | Irish Parliament formed after Sinn Fein election victory. |
| **1919-1921** | War between Irish Republican Army and British Army. |
| **1922** | Irish Free State founded, while six northern counties remain part of United Kingdom as Northern Ireland, or Ulster; civil war up until 1923 between rival republican groups. |
| **1949** | Foundation of Irish Republic after all remaining constitutional links with Britain are severed. |